AF608377

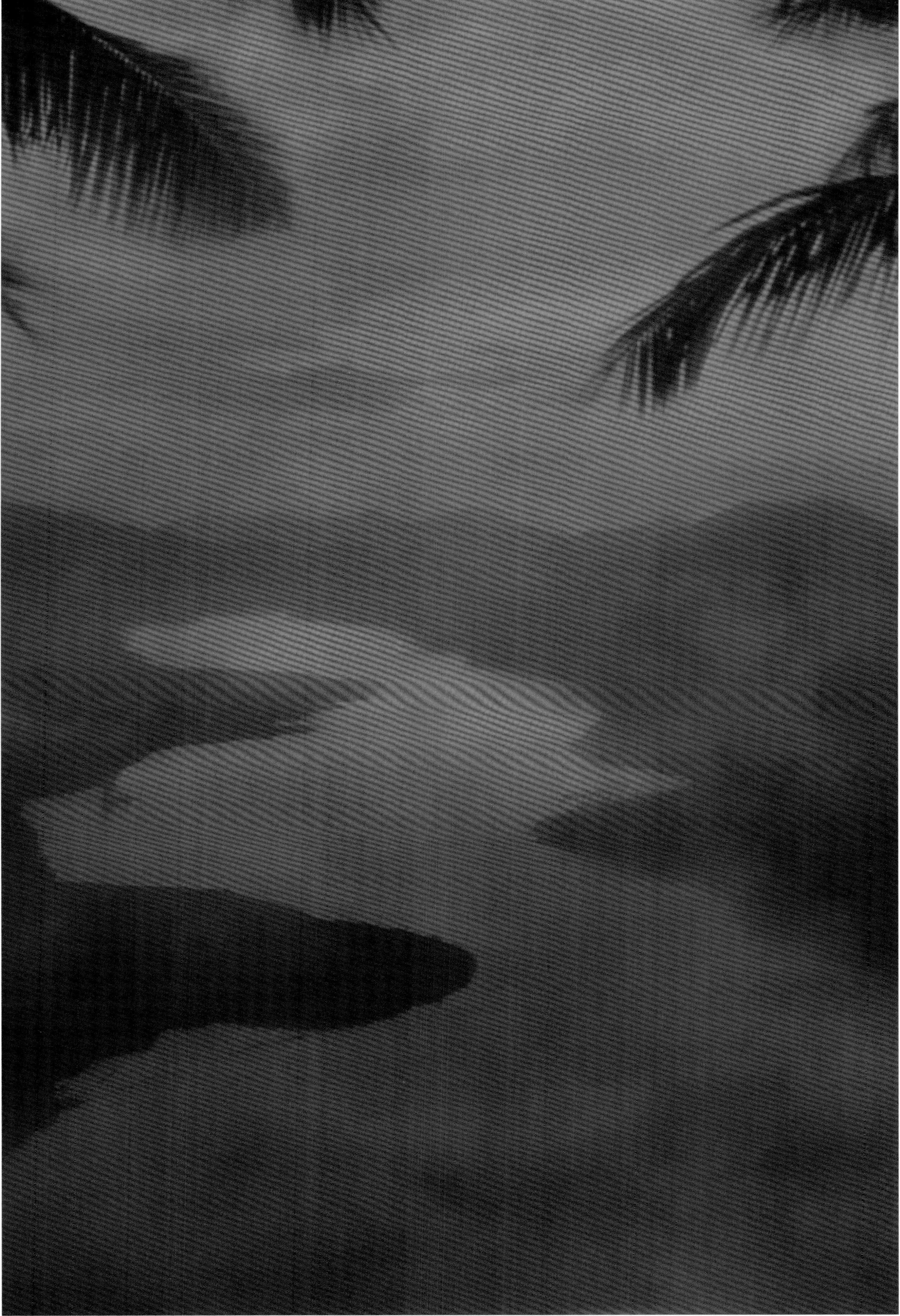

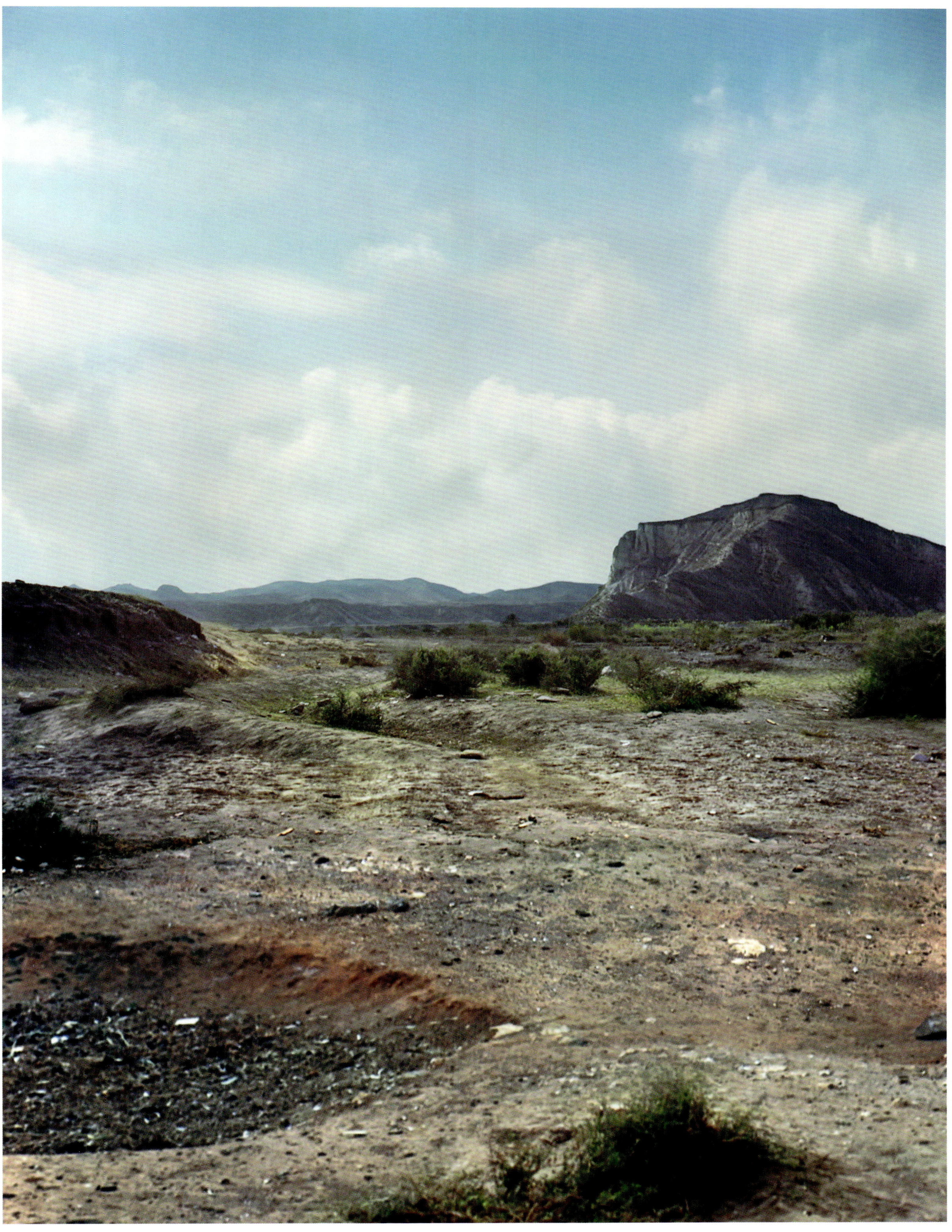

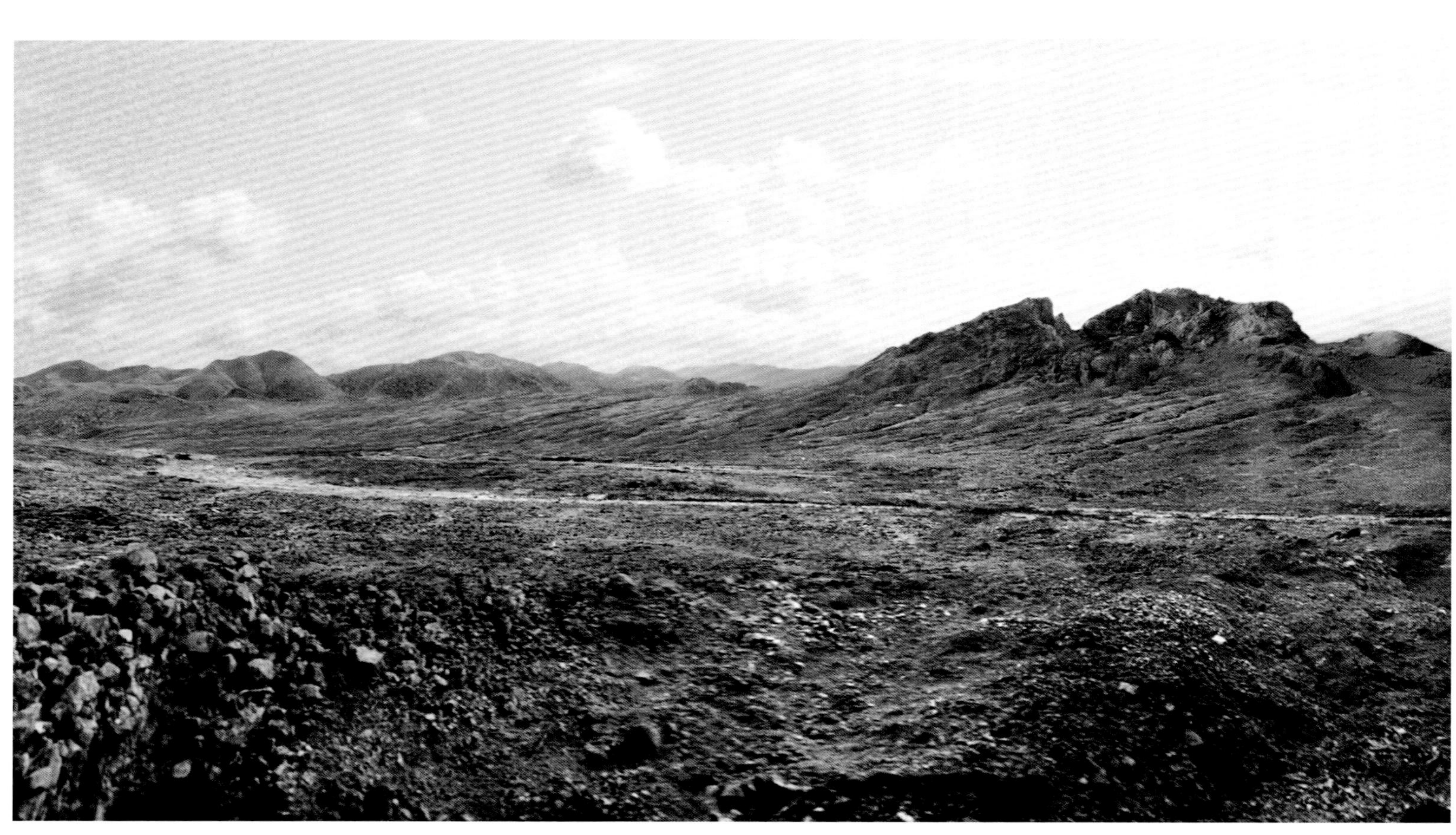

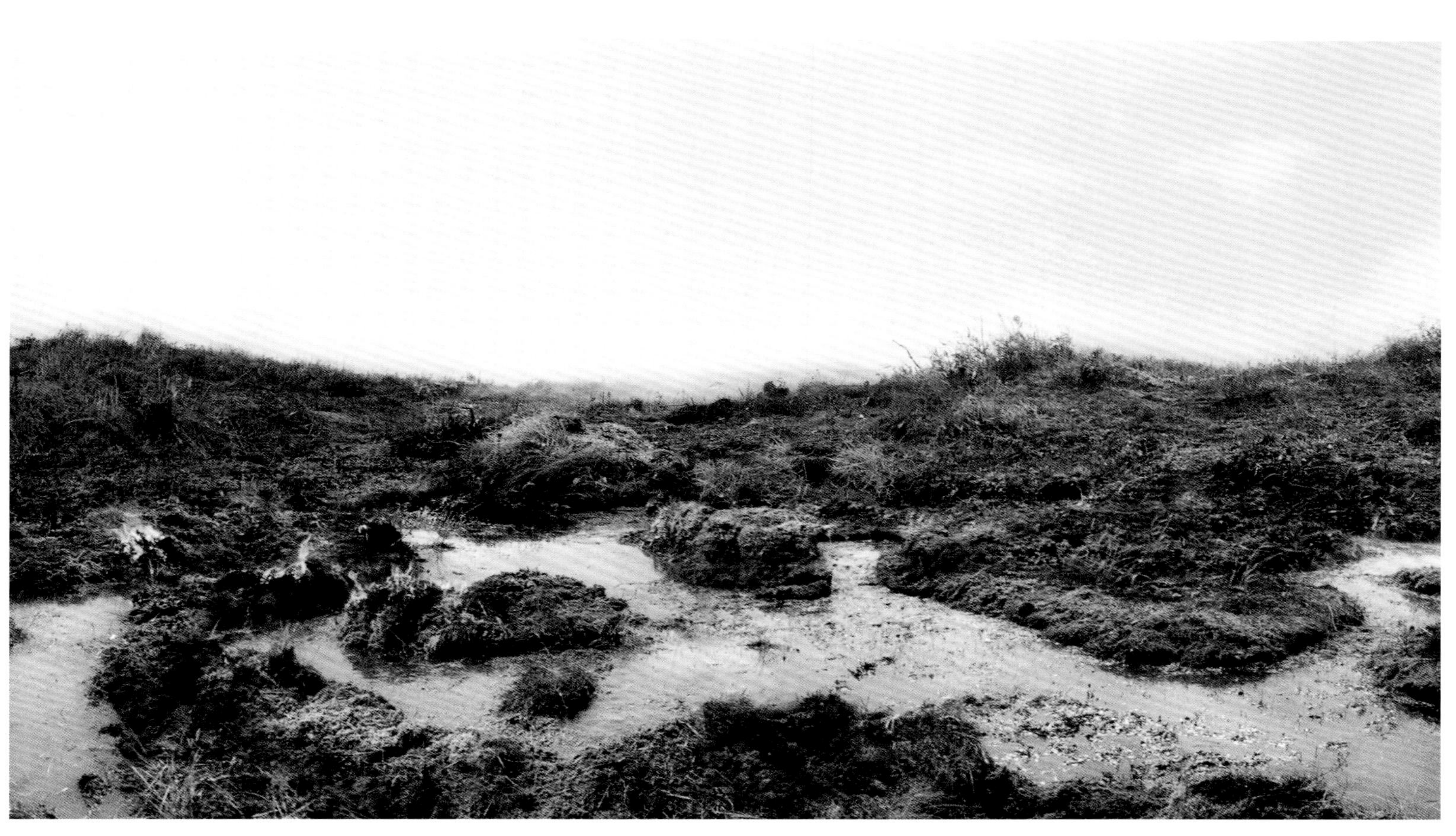

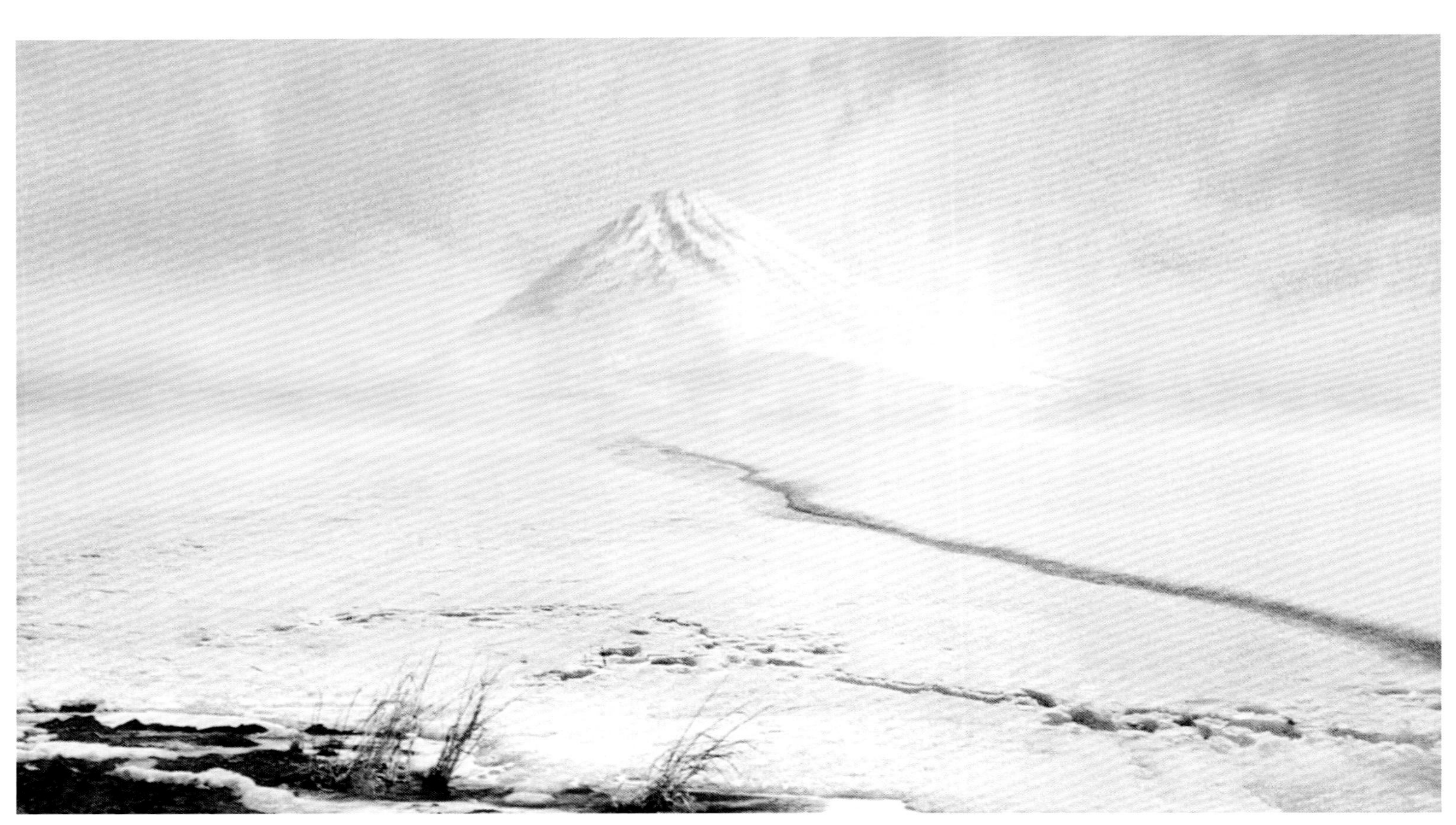

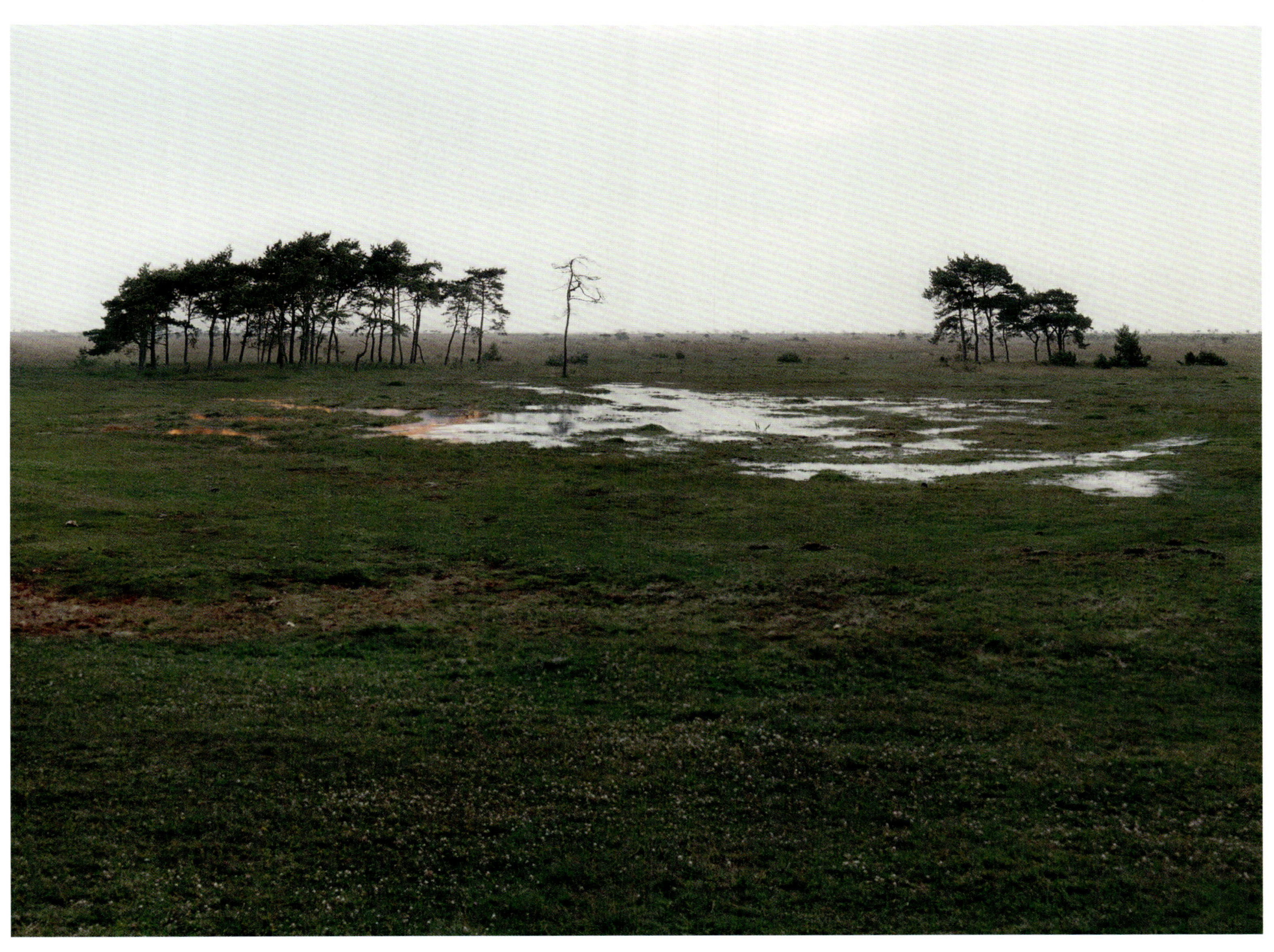

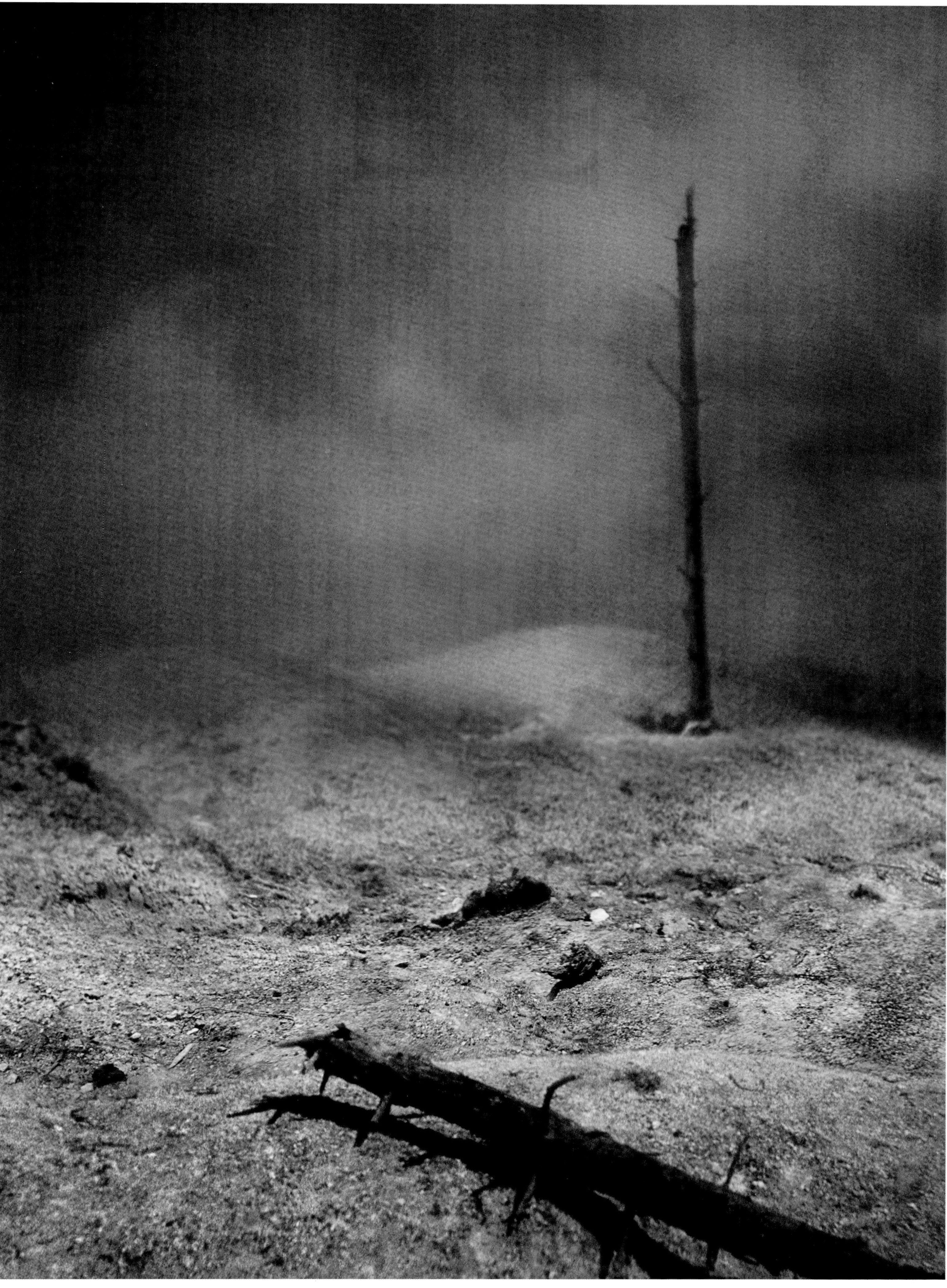

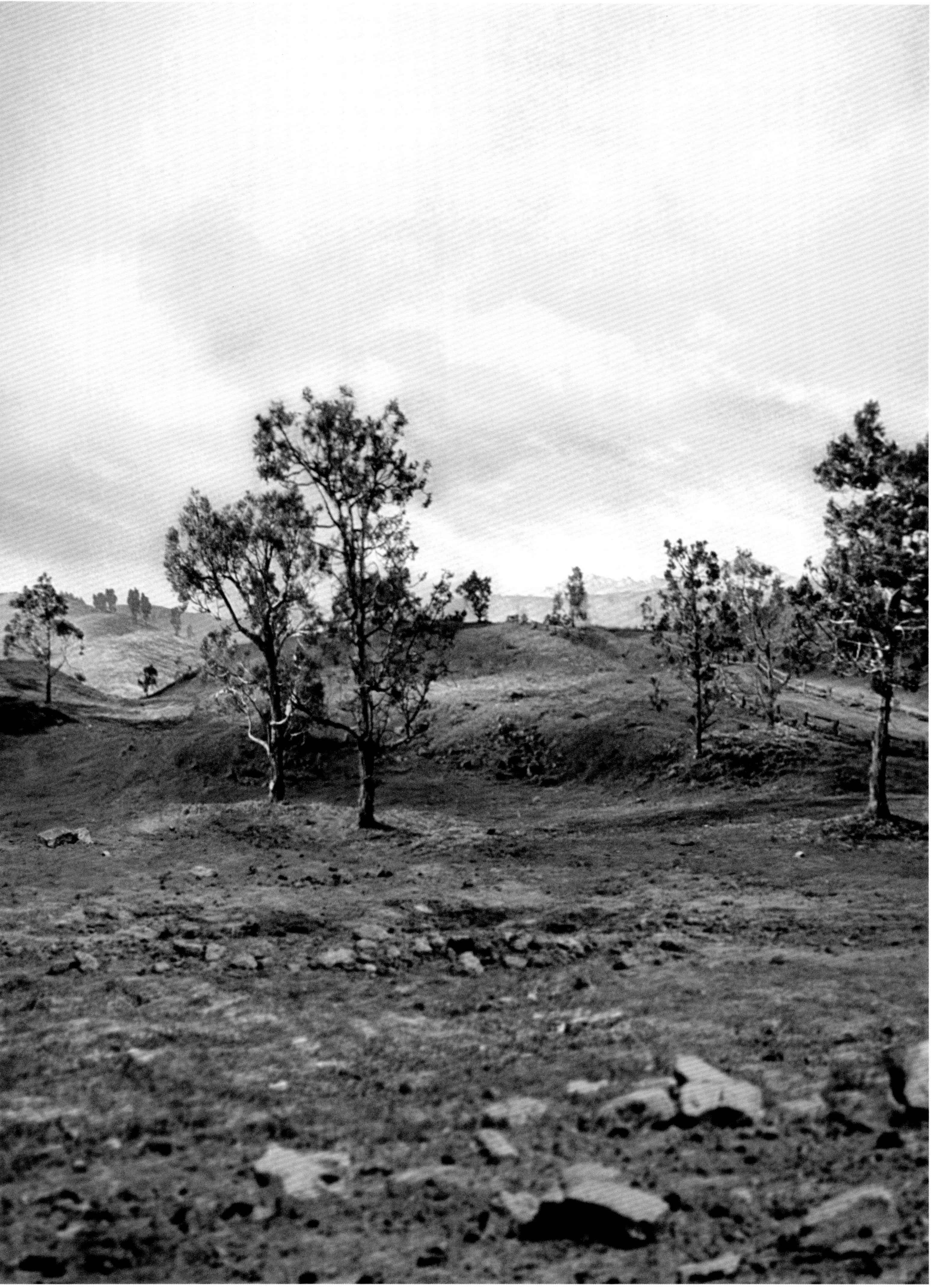

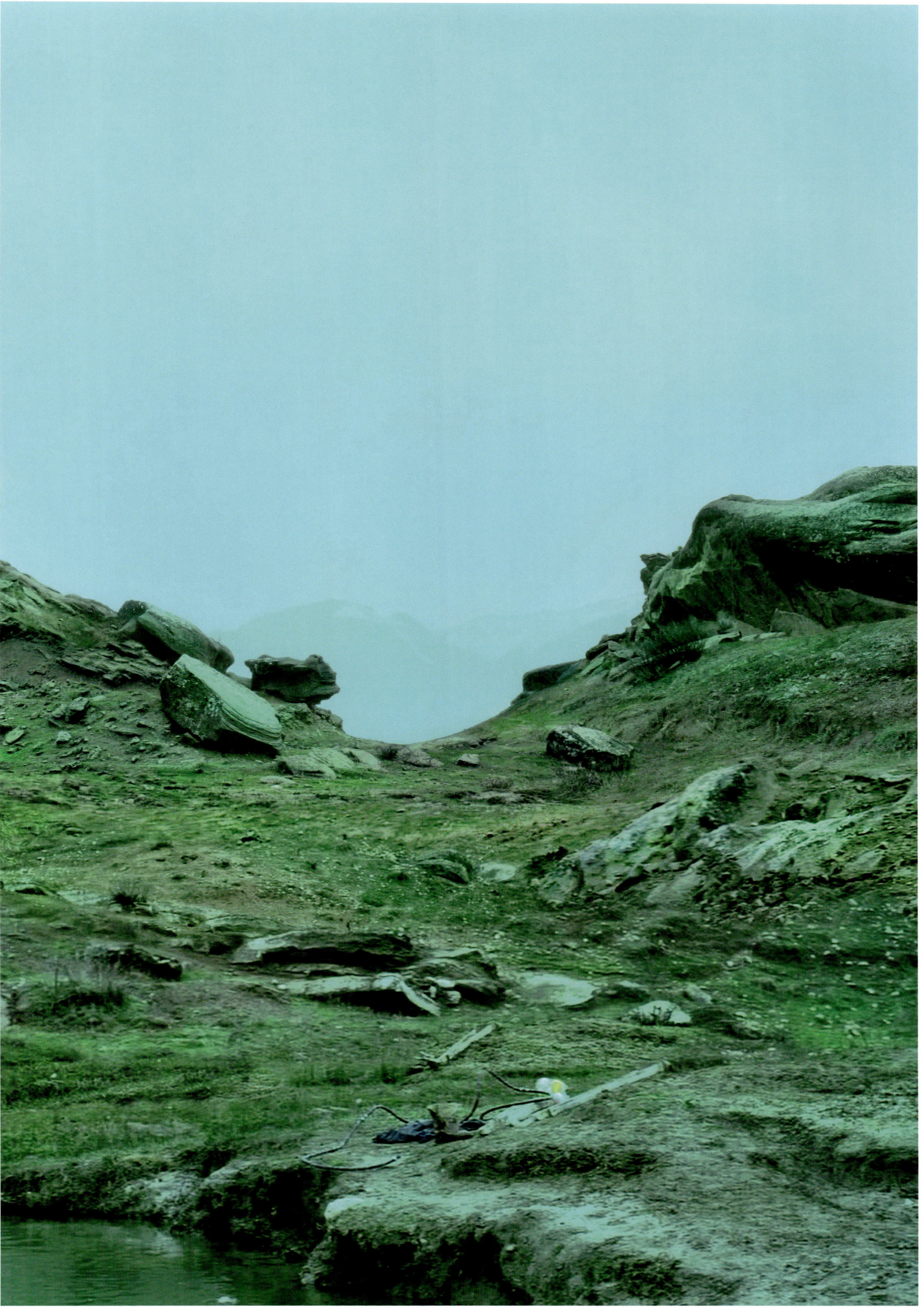

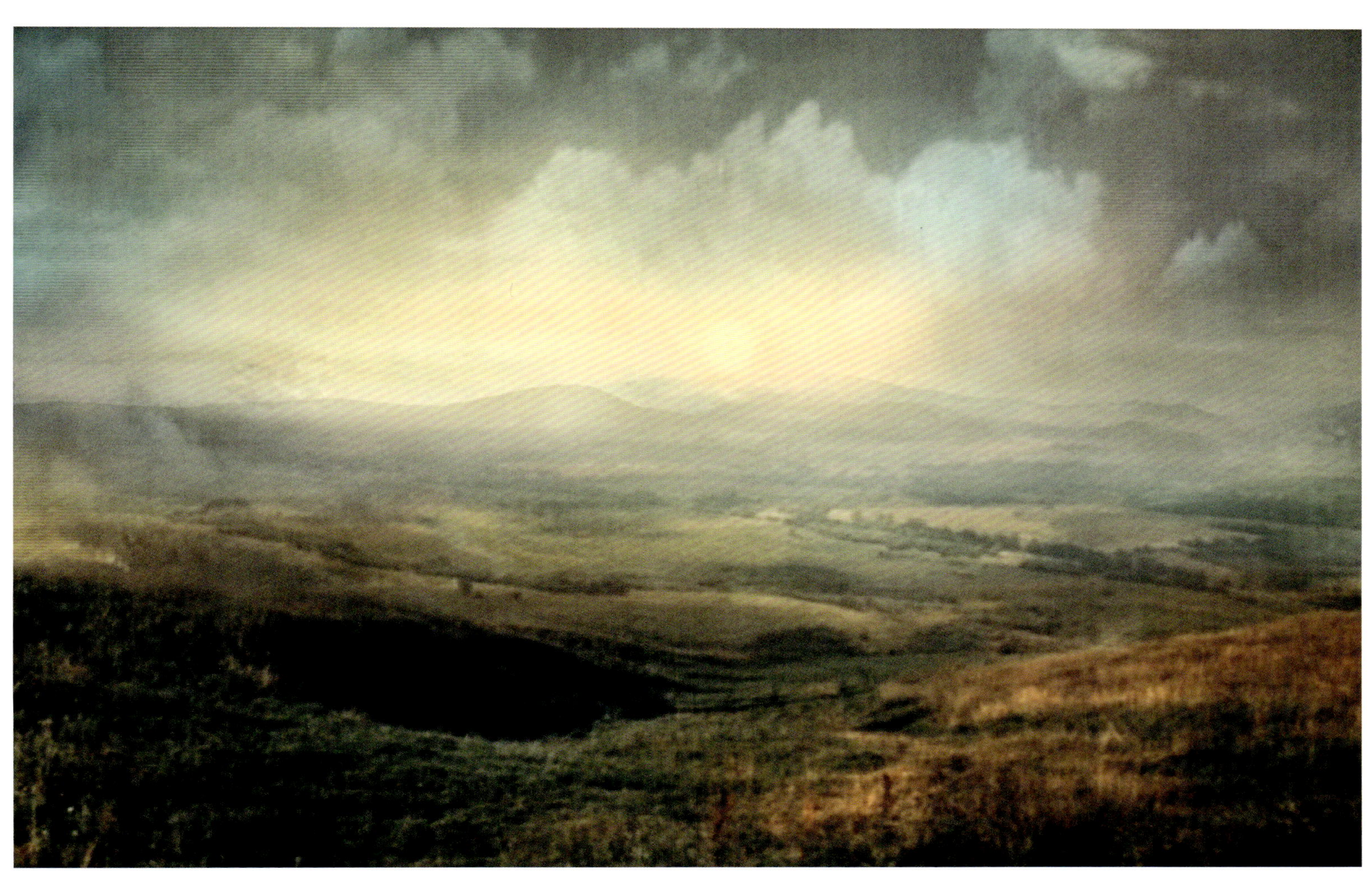

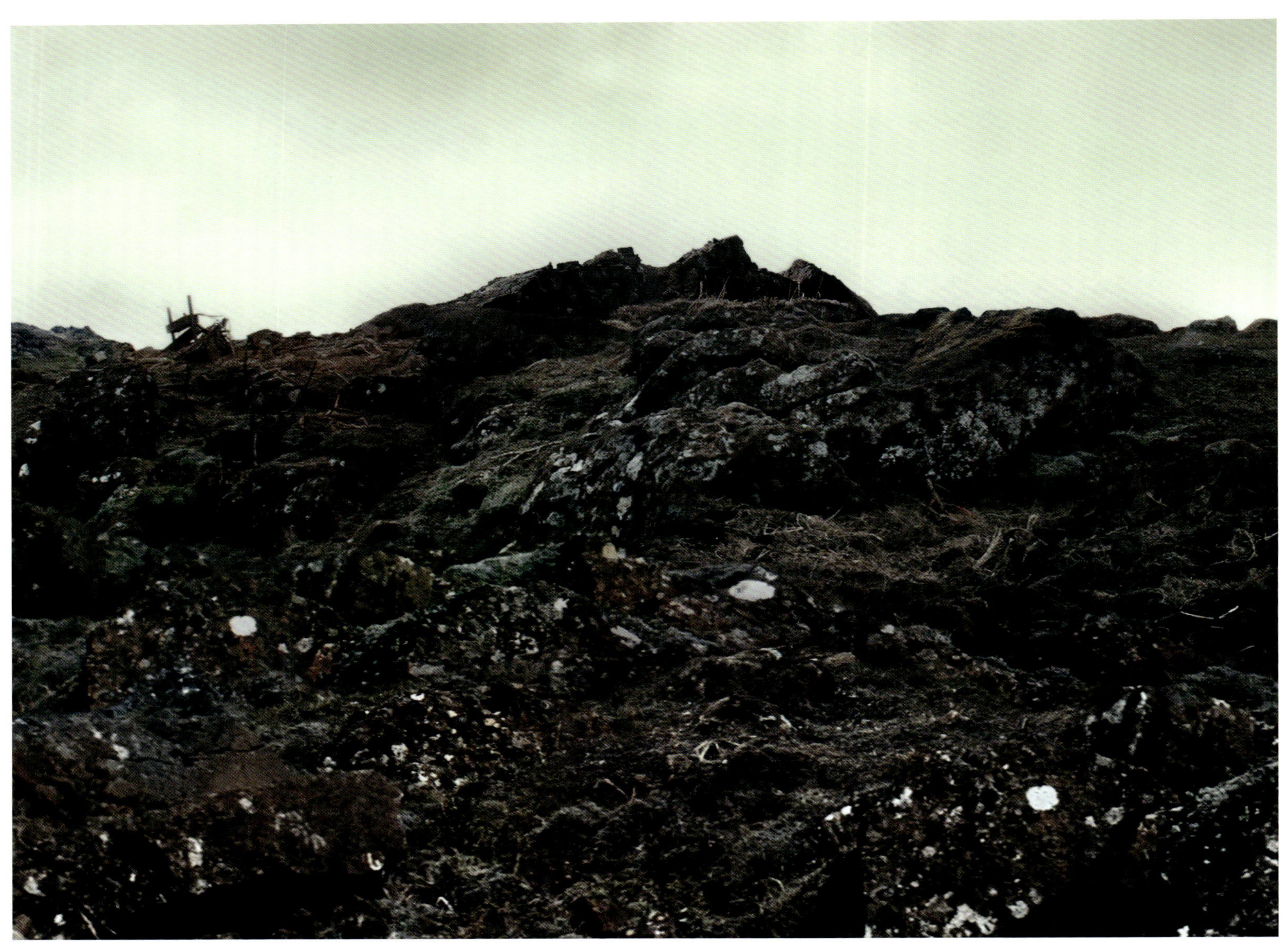

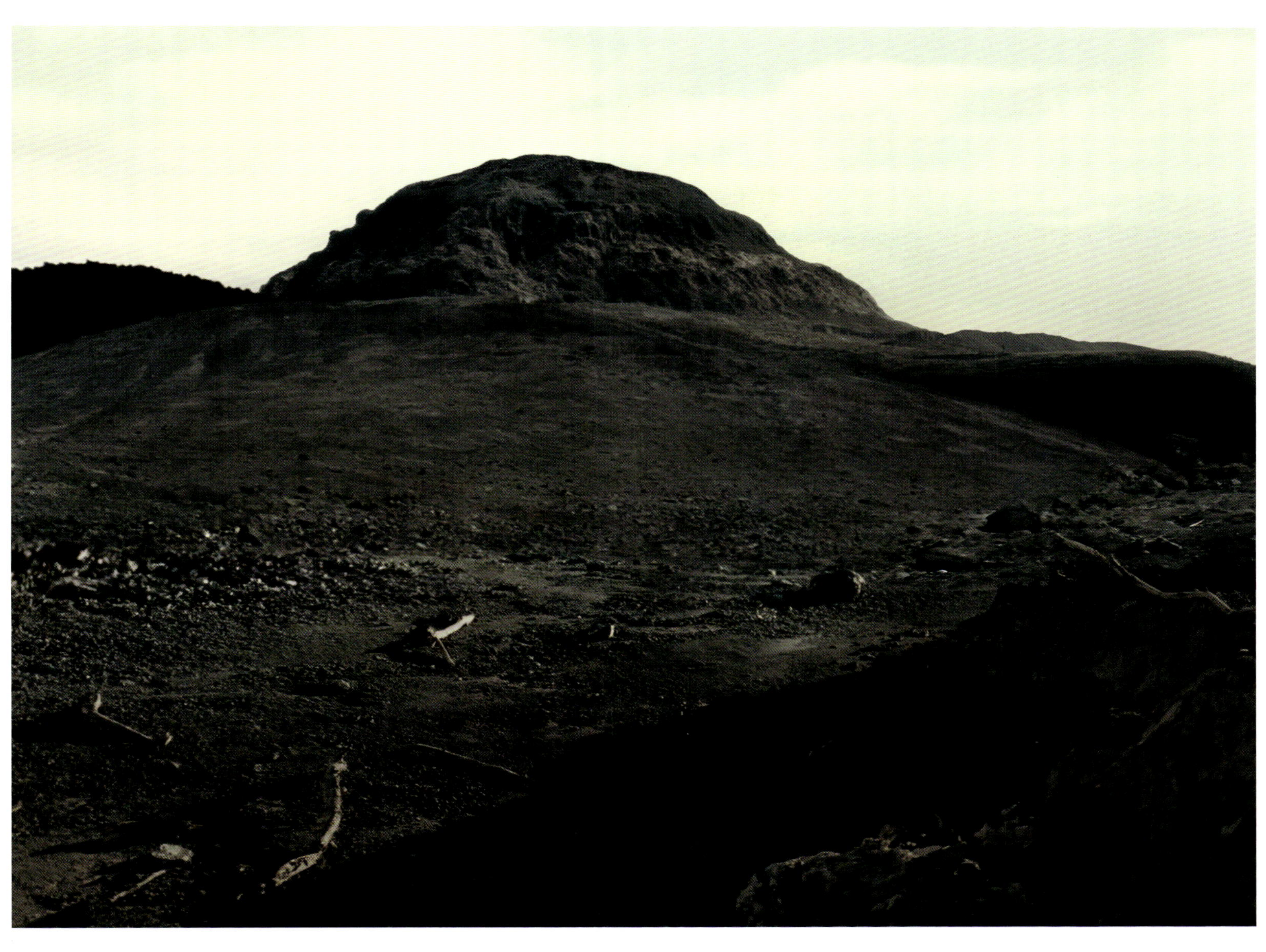

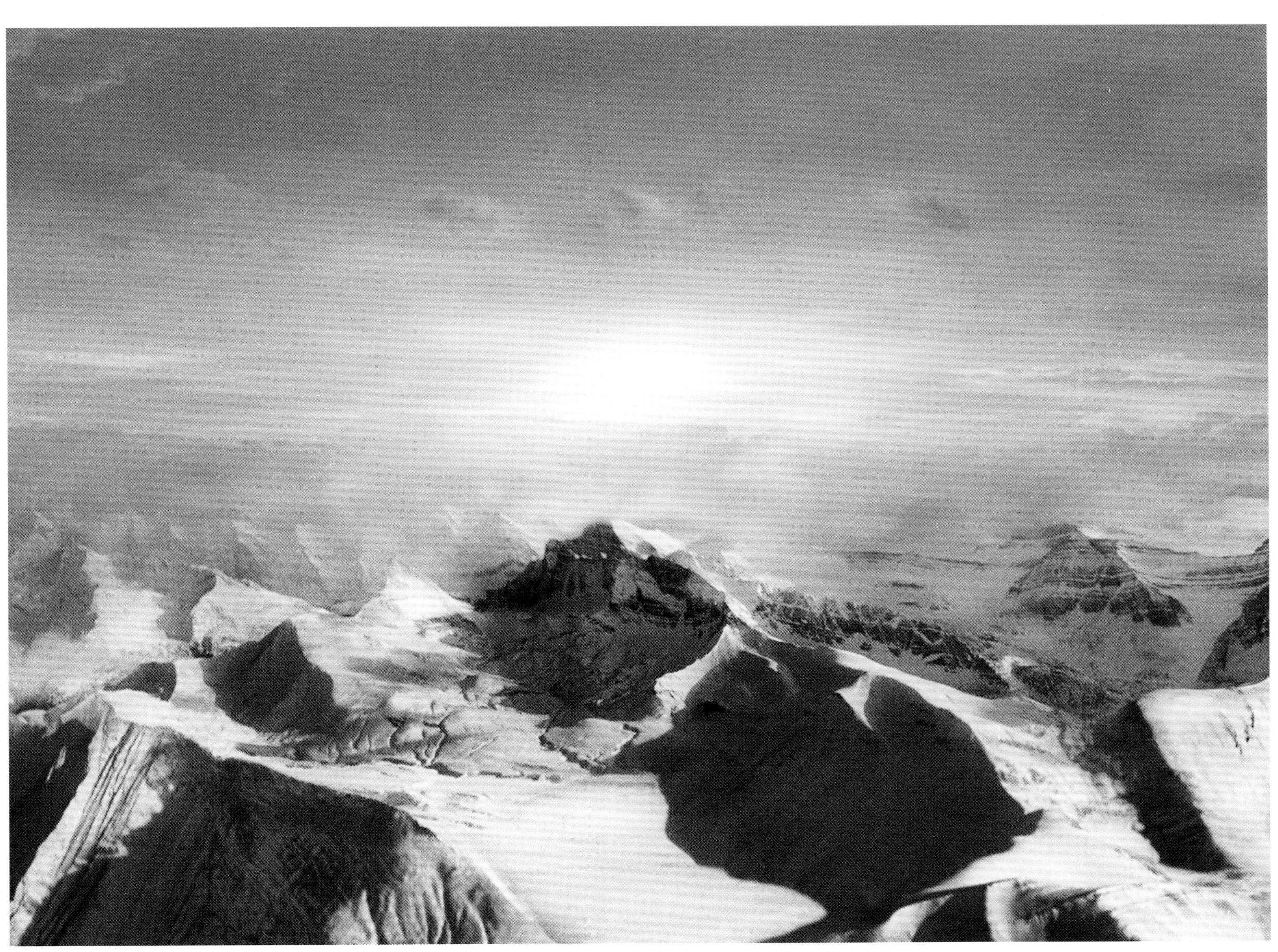

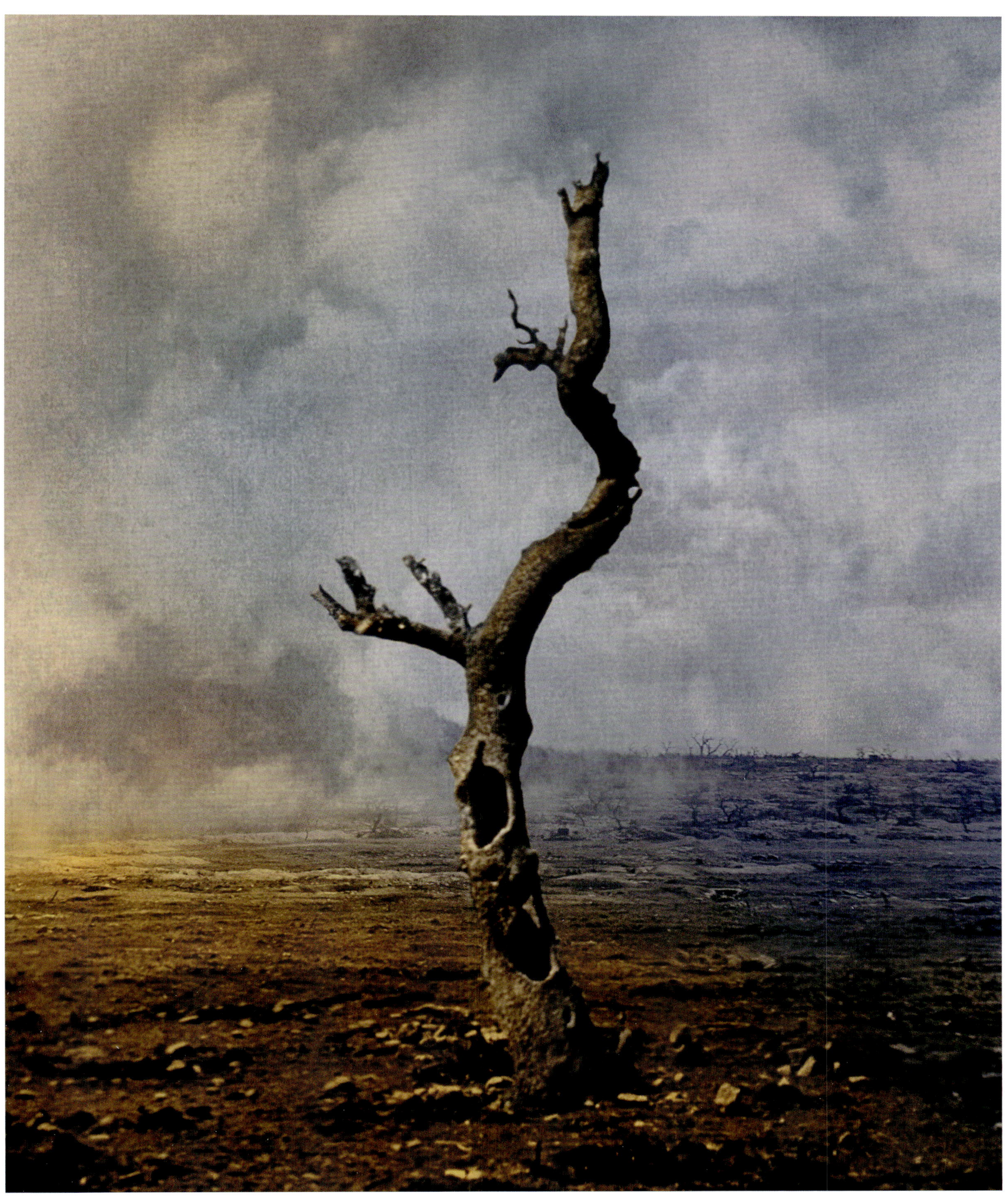

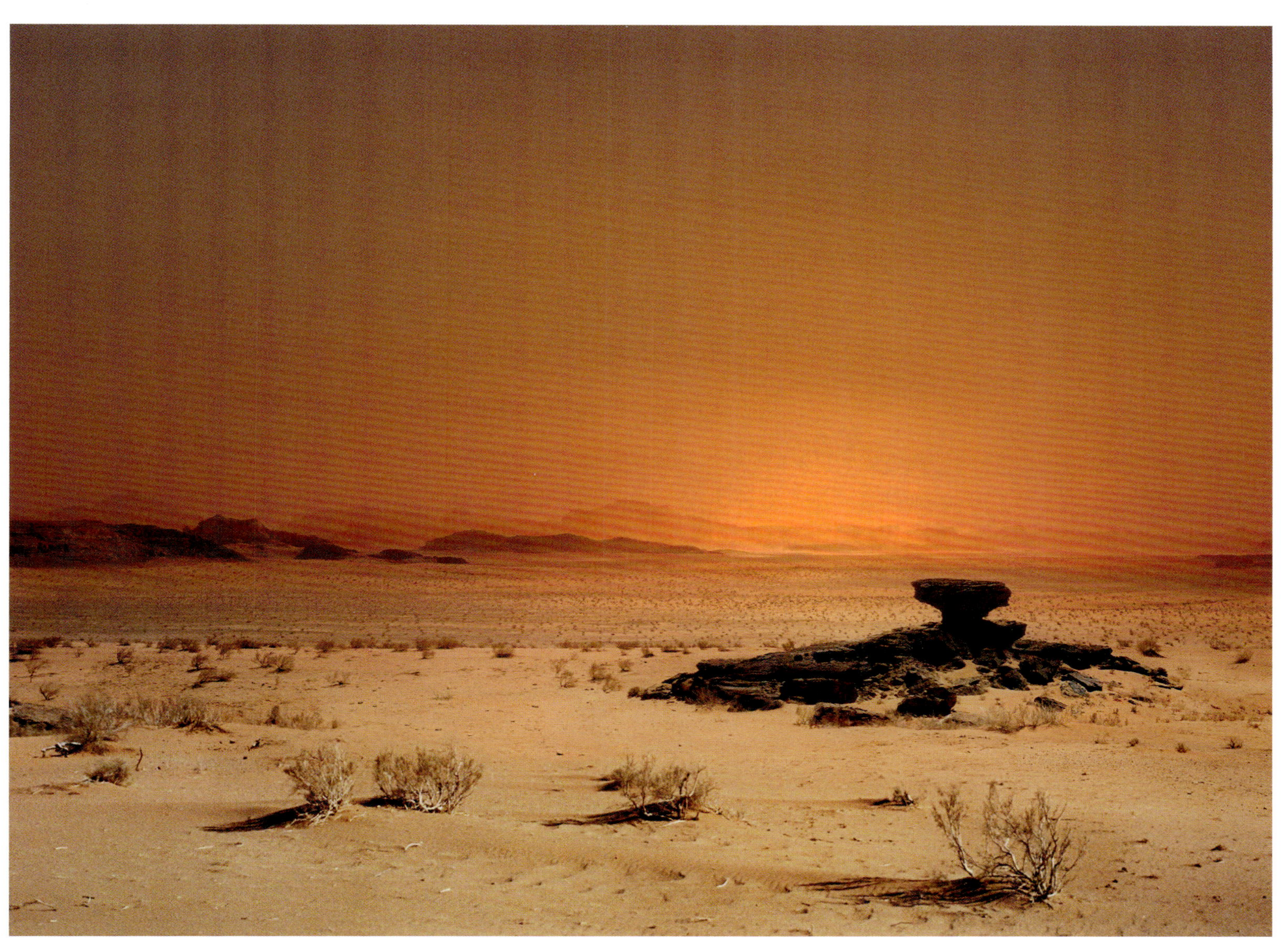

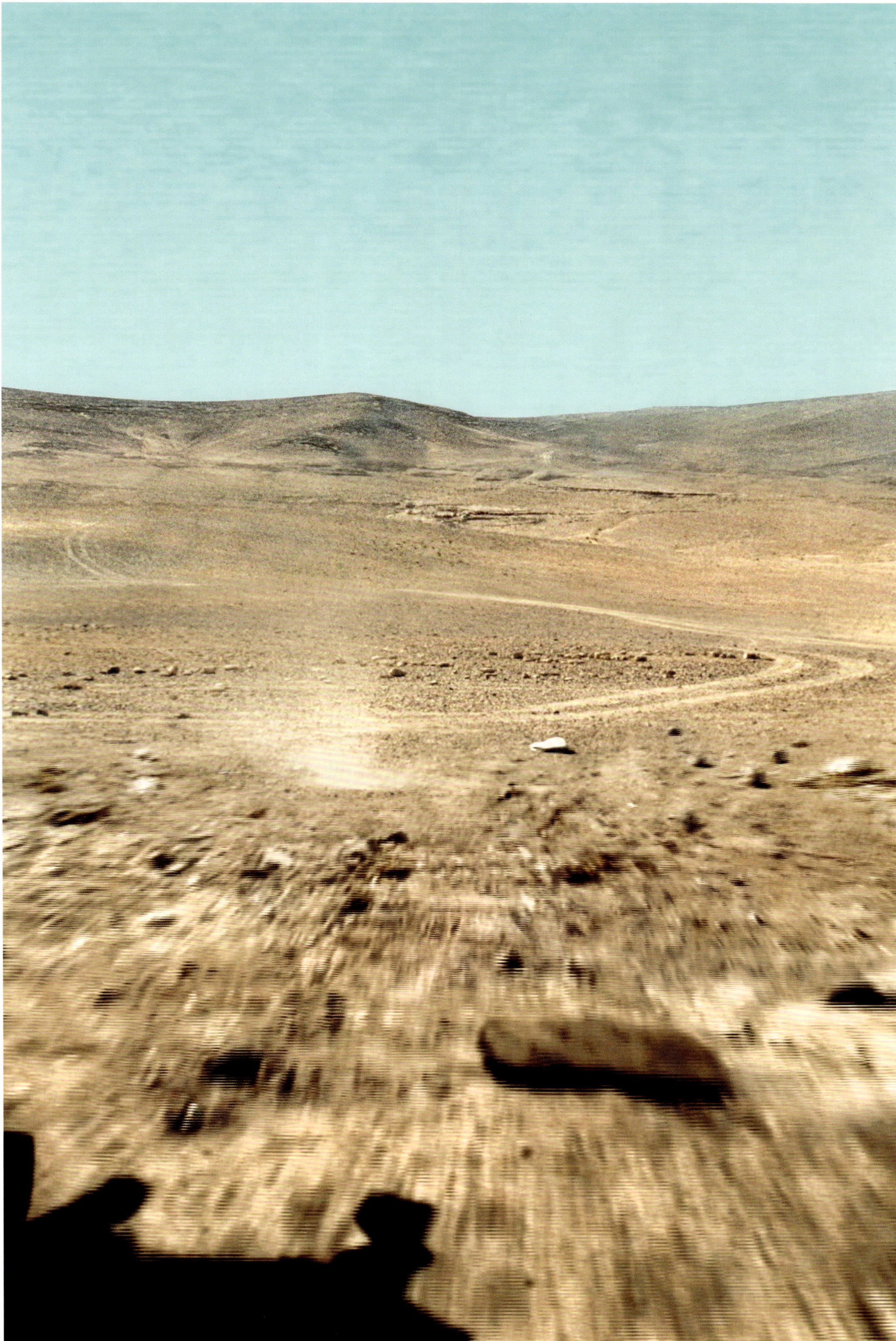

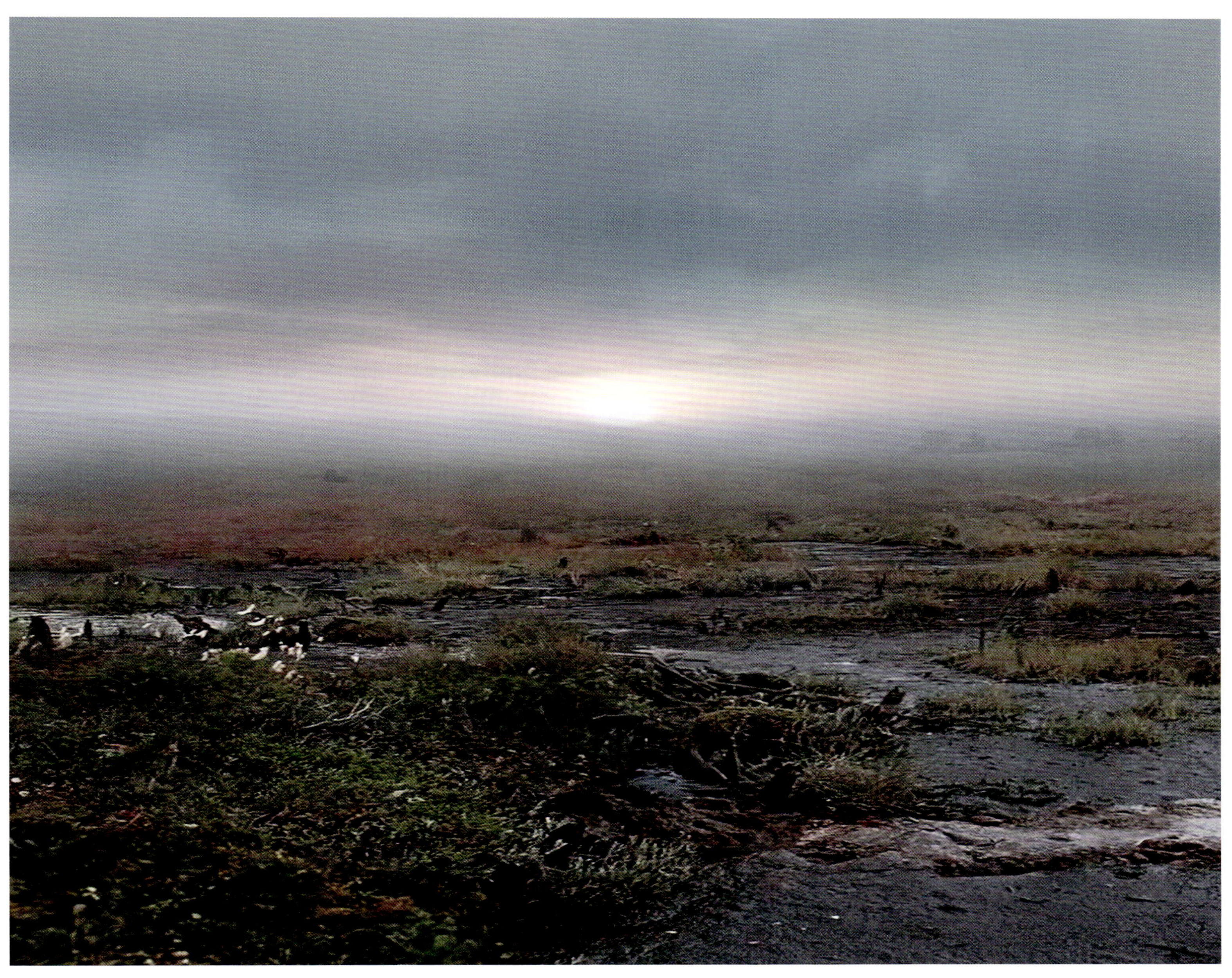

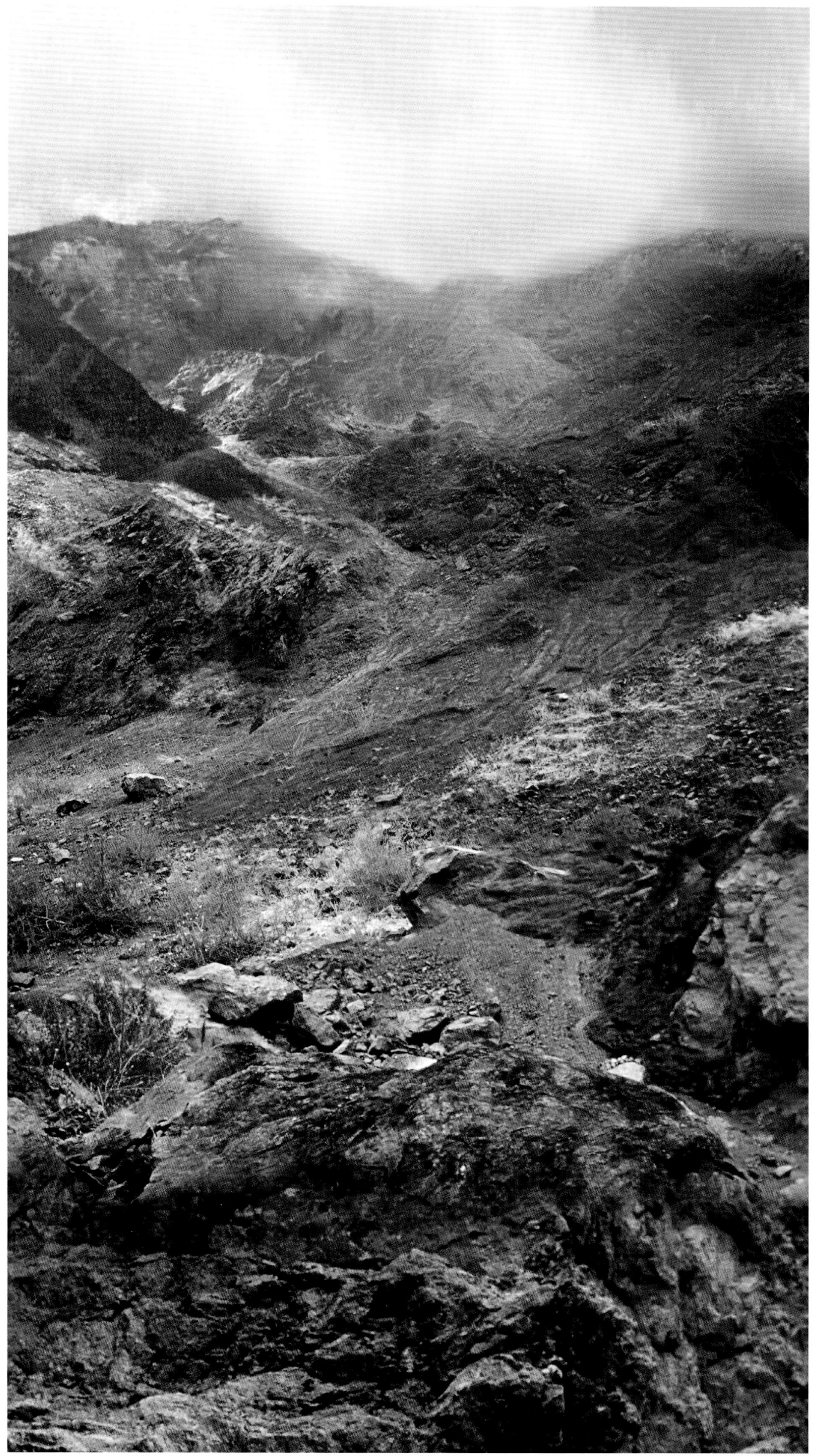

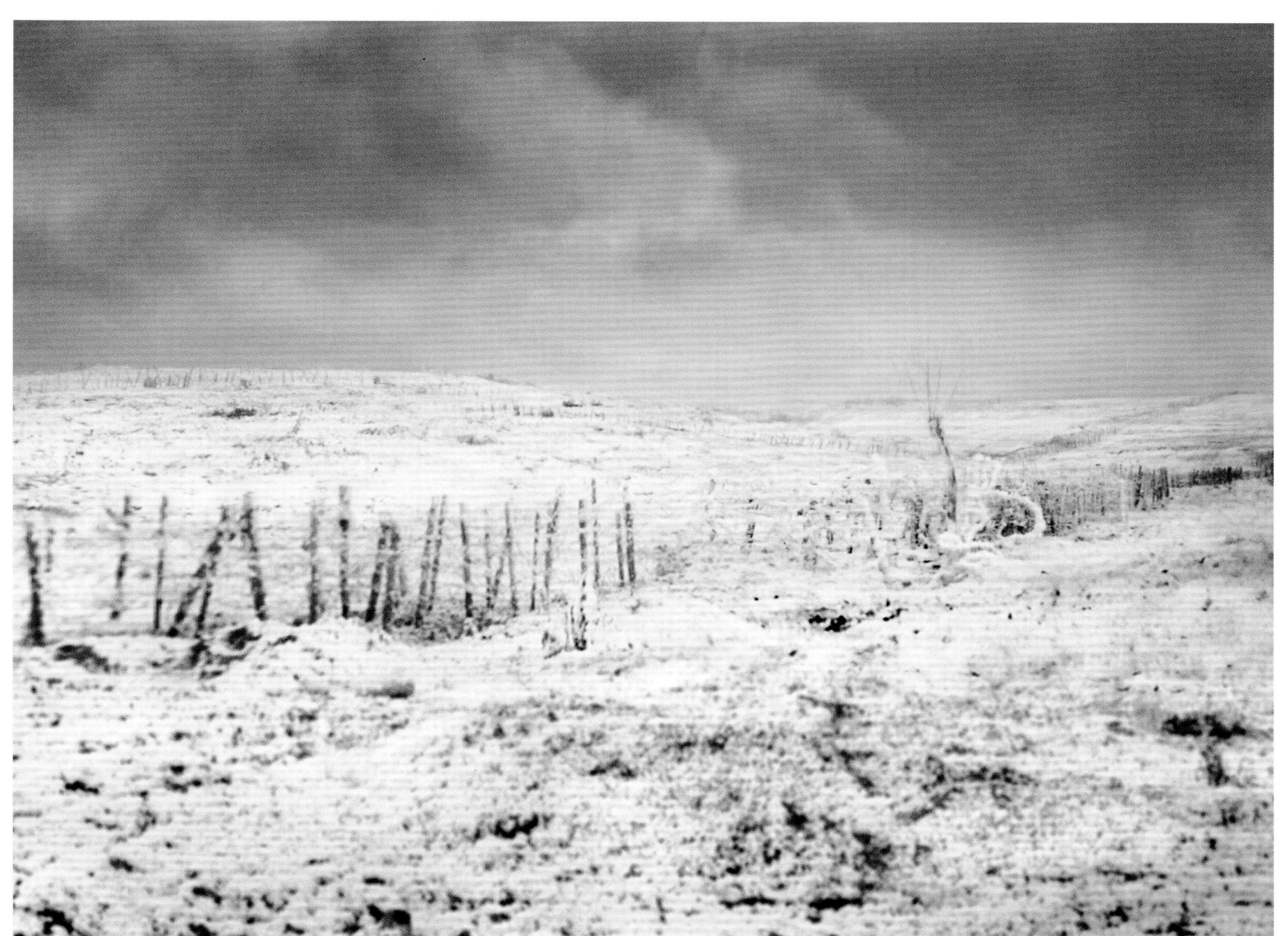

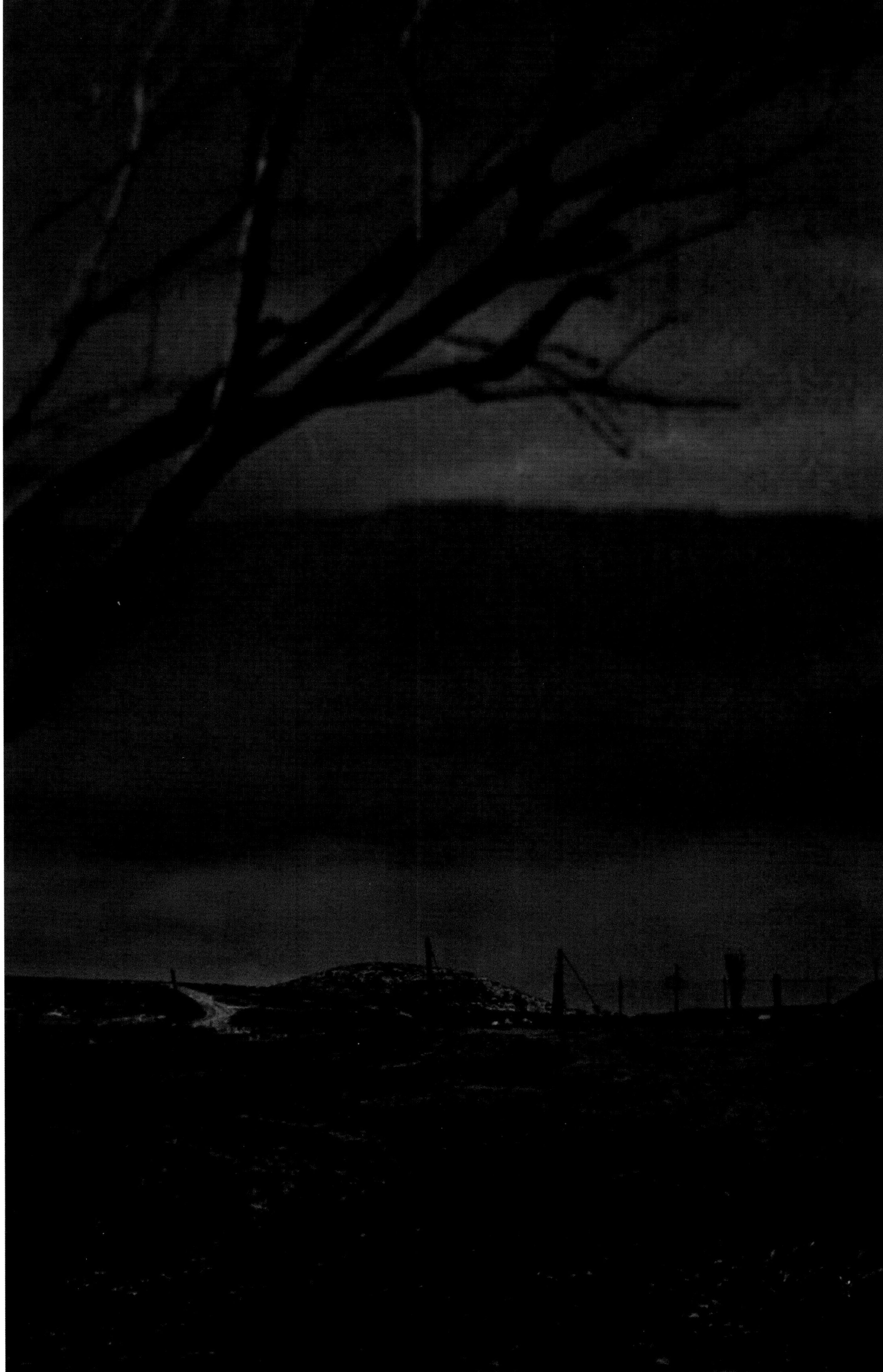

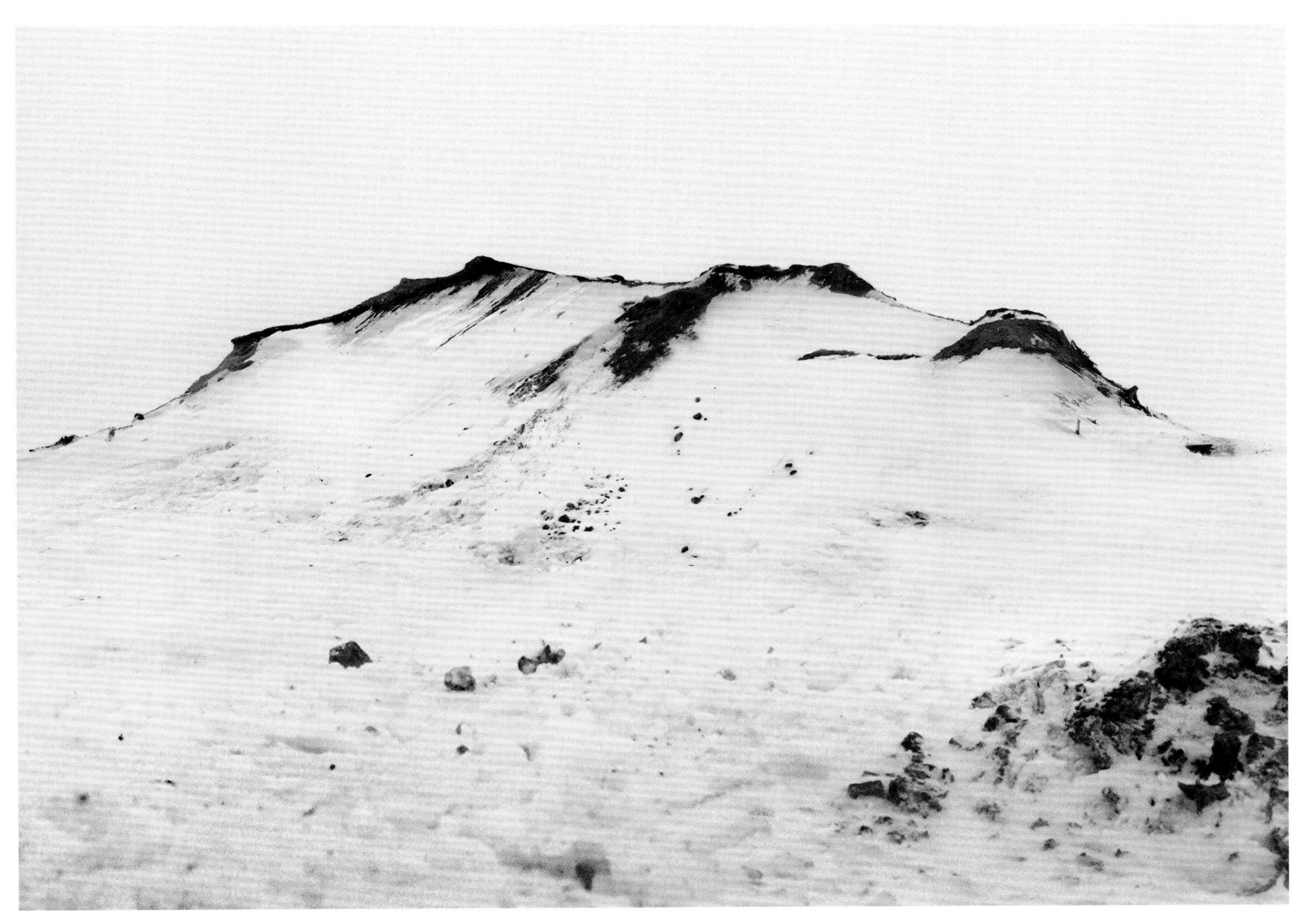

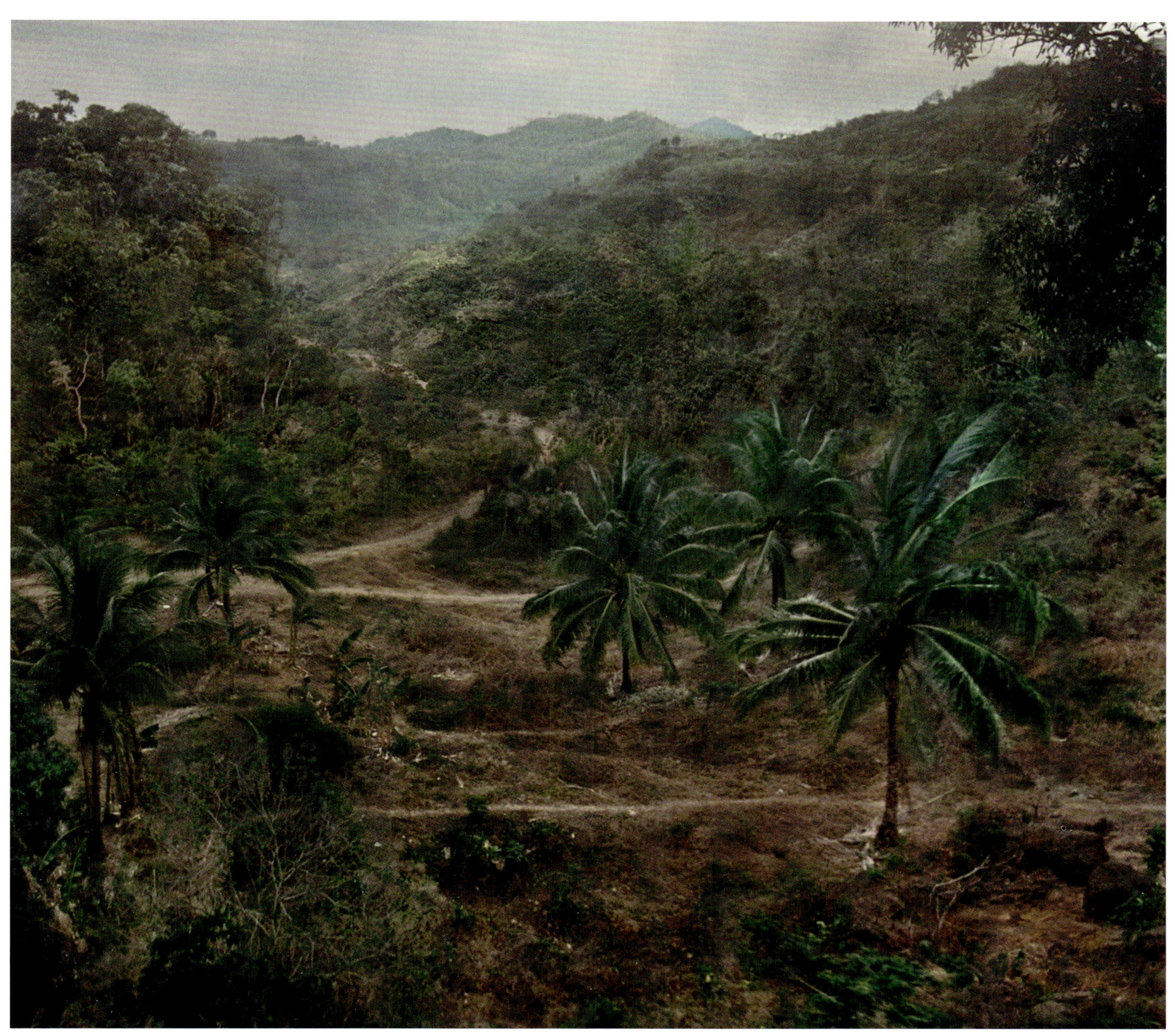

Apocalypse Now
Patton
The Human Condition
(I No Greater Love)
The Human Condition
(II Road to Eternity)
The Human Condition
(III A Soldiers
Prayer)
Sacrifice
Wooden Crosses
The Great Dictator
Turtles Can Fly
War and Peace
Battleship Potemkin
Paths of Glory
Flags Of Our Fathers
Letters From Iwo Jima
Dr Strangelove
Wings
Lawrence of Arabia
The Hurt Locker
Come and See
Men in War
Oh What A Lovely War
Army of Shadows
Stalingrad
Platoon

DAVID CAMPANY IN CONVERSATION WITH MORTEN BARKER

David: Morten to begin with, could you say at little about the origins of the *Terra Nullius* series? Was it clear from the start what you had in mind?

Morten: The very first thoughts to do with *Terra Nullius* came during my projects with Danish military landscapes, in 2013. Back then I was handed the video footage from the target camera of a Danish Leopard tank. Most of it shows a gun turret's constant sweeping of the "enemy" landscapes from left to right, and right to left. It is monotonous footage, which fascinated me and sparked the idea of combining it into one single landscape image without a clear geography, depth of field or time. This was much inspired by Hiroshi Sugimoto's *Movie Theaters* project where he embedded an entire film's duration into a single image. Also during this time I was constantly watching war movies, and while viewing Letyat Zhuravli's *The Cranes are Flying* from 1957 I immediately connected the idea from the Leopard tank with taking the dolly movements from the film, and turning these too into a single landscape image. In reality I never could get *The Cranes are Flying* to work, but the thought stayed with me. Then in the spring of 2016, I was going to take part in a small group exhibition, and I decided to attempt to make one film landscape work. The film I began working on was Anthony Mann's *Men in War,* also from 1957. After a month of numerous screenshots, lots of digital montage and stitching I succeeded in creating a single landscape image that I felt happy about. From then on I began buying and collecting war films on DVD and Blu-Ray and made the decision to make a series of works. Thus *Terra Nullius* began.

David: Already this is a rich set of concepts! The re-imagining of space and time. The slippage between war, memory of war and war as image. The compression of narrative into a single image. The compression of complex geographies into single landscapes. Do you work to a plan for each image in the series?

Morten: It is not so much a plan as it is a series of repetitive work steps. After 'screen-shotting' every landscape scene I begin stitching camera movements and selected scenes, and digitally removing the human presence. It is quite monotonous work, but it provides me with a library of empty landscapes. Then follows the actual process of sketching and montage. This is a chaotic process of frustration and discovery: assembling screenshot fragments, cloning textures, applying colours, enlarging and shrinking pixels. The final image is achieved when the landscape possesses its own space while still retaining something of the original movie's tension, narration and time.

One of the struggles with working on *Terra Nullius* was not to think of them as photographs but to let the constant manipulation of pixels, colour casts, and ever changing depths of field shape each image. This part of the process has proved highly liberating.

I work with one constraint or rule. The height or width of each image is determined by the widest camera movement or panning in each film. For example, in *Lawrence of Arabia* the width of the final image was determined by stitching the screenshots from the camera pan when Lawrence gathers the Arab tribes and they begin the long journey across the desert. When stitched and printed in 200 dpi this gave the image a width of 128 cm.

The project is as much about finding a way to work with memory. I never felt I could examine memory through photography; because memory is fallible and imprecise. But a film I could view as a compressed narration of life. And so by using film I could conduct my own fragmented experiments and maybe find the landscapes of my childhood. A landscape that I never saw, but psychologically contains fear, violence and isolation.

David: I sense the remaking of the memory of a film in terms of your own subjective experience of landscape belongs to what is actually a long tradition of artists reversing the psychological dynamic between the narrative film and the viewer. Instead of subjecting oneself to the film, the film is subjected to the will of one's self. I think of André Breton and Jacques Vaché in the 1920s, getting up and leaving a movie theater as soon as they were bored, walking down the road and diving into another one, assembling their own movie from the fragments they saw. Much later we have the film still collages of John Stezaker and John Baldessari. But 'mashinema' is now a popular genre on YouTube, where anyone can reedit a movie.

Morten: There is a feeling of "taking control" not so much of the narrative but of the individual frames in a sort of image taxonomy. In the process of breaking up each movie into its individual frames and reassembling them into a single landscape there is a distancing for the spectator that both uncovers the illusion of cinema as a mere succession of still images and of memory as an illusion of the brain created by bits and pieces of perception. Its subsequent meaning is the acknowledgement that my search for my childhood nightmarish landscapes is an artistic illusion and an impossible quest for a "truth". Projecting the movie's imagery onto a single cartographic landscape *Terra Nullius* shifts back and forth between the subjective search for a landscape and the objective approach in front of Photoshop. When working with each individual frame it feels like re-shaping the movie narrative. No different from Hugo Munsterberg's observations in *The Photoplay:* "We do not see the objective reality, but a product of our own mind which binds the pictures together."

Throughout the work on *Terra Nullius* there has always existed an underlying intellectual and perhaps superstitious belief that each of the twenty-four movies possesses a singular landscape waiting to get out. A bit like an abstract reversal of Wim Wenders quote: *"Every photo is the first frame of a film".* The thought must originate from knowing Sugimoto's *Movie Theatre* series. In *Terra Nullius* I work by reversal. I work backwards by recreating the "Image of the Void", refilling an empty Photoshop screen with my own subjective and fragmented memory, and recreating a new movie landscape that contains and interprets the movie's narrative.

One of the projects that has stuck with me is Joan Fontcuberta's *Orogenesis* in which he creates digital landscapes by feeding software with famous paintings by Monet, Gaugin and others. I have enjoyed the idea that the same could be accomplished with *Terra Nullius.* That by feeding each of the twenty-four movies into software and having it run through its algorithms it too could punch out a single landscape.

David: I often wonder if still photographers are haunted by the promise of narrative, and perhaps simply duration, that are really beyond them, while filmakers are haunted by the opposite, the single image that promises to express it all. Perhaps a project such as *Terra Nullius* comes from somewhere between those two.

Morten: I remember the impact of seeing Chris Marker's film *La Jetée* for the first time and feeling the joy of being immersed in the cinematic narrative of photographs. There was also a sense of movement because the duration of each photograph never held long enough on screen for my gaze to become fixed on any certain place. The flickering frame rate of cinema magically gave the illusion of movement. It reminds me of when I was a child and we were given cardboard wrist clocks with hands drawn by marker pen.

My memory is still that the hands moved! I know *La Jetée* has been influential to my thinking through of *Terra Nullius* and perhaps my next work will get me closer to something that is between the photographic and cinematic.

David: Like Marker's *La Jetée, Terra Nullius* is another reminder of the richness and expanse of this territory between photography and cinema, and between the still and the moving image. Very often our first assumption is that is a really tight and particular space, when in fact a great deal of our experience of images, and a great deal of the important art of the last century comes from precisely this space - hybrid, in-between, not belonging clearly to one thing or another. It's not anti-modernist exactly, because very often the work does have a modernist impulse to explore the nature and parameters of mediums, and make audiences think about them, but it does so by stepping out of the familiar categories and expectations. Beyond this of course, there is the nature of subjective experience, memory, the unconscious and involuntary recall, which you just mentioned. It seems to me this territory between stillness and movement is actually a very helpful space in which to explore such experience because it shares similar structures, similar spatial and temporal instabilities.

Morten: Perhaps the reason why the space in-between is so enticing is because it floats and drifts between. It accentuates differences and similarities and so it holds a promise to be its own. Perhaps this is how memory works; it to floats and drifts between the objective and subjective. This is the immediate allure of the space to me as it holds a promise of a kind of genealogy of my subjective memory.

Exploring the space in-between has also become a working process that has liberated me from the technical considerations of taking photographs. I no longer have to participate in the technical aspects of photography. No more shutter speed, aperture, contrast, white balance etc., because the cinematographers, directors and colourists have already made those decisions for me. What is left for me is to combine the technology of screen-shotting and the white canvas of Photoshop in creating landscapes. It has brought about a newfound freedom as a photographer. It also means I can leave the nostalgia of the darkroom behind; a space I have always found both magical and frustrating. The magic is seeing the image appear in the developer. The frustration is the slowness of the process. The digital space and its immediate response suit my impatience even though it means the magic has gone.

The project has also solved the long-time frustration with camera dependency and consumption. I remember very early on the allure of owning a Hasselblad—mostly because of two notches it left on the negative or the Leica Digilux 1, which was my first digital camera, and made me part of digital technology; but the cameras I have owned have not changed my visual vocabulary. I spent a lot of time imagining that my artistic expression was dependent on a technical device. With *Terra Nullius* this dependency is almost non-existent. I am free from photographic gadgetry, and from taking photos. Instead I have discovered a new visual language among the existing photographic and cinematic material. This is one of the reasons the space is so interesting, and perhaps it offers a new way of being a photographer.

David: It's interesting that you think of this process as pursuing photography by other means. But what if you had come to this process through being a filmmaker, or movie editor? What if you'd come to it from painting? Would you still think of it as photography? I agree that it's a radically hybrid field you're operating in, but I'm intrigued by your holding onto the idea of being a photographer here.

Morten: Two painters have made me question the medium of photography and made me believe there are other means by which to take photographs. One is Gerhard Richter and his photo-paintings, of which he said: "I'm not trying to imitate a photograph; I'm trying to make one. And if I disregard the assumption that a photograph is a piece of paper exposed to light, then I am practicing photography by other means." His work is inseparable from photography. The other is David Hockney and in particular his work *Pearblossom Highway.* It is a collage of multiple Polaroids taken from separate perspectives to better reflect the way the human eye sees the world. I am quite intrigued by his general distrust of photography and his opposition to the single vanishing point of classical Renaissance perspective. Both Hockney's and Richter's views on the medium are inspiring. Maybe it is because they do not feel any loyalty to the camera or nostalgia for the history of photography.

I do not know when I first gave thought to the wonder that when pressing the keyboard shortcut to take a screenshot it makes the sound of the camera shutter. At one point I took screenshots of live feeds from weather stations and surveillance cameras and I regarded that action to be equal to holding a camera and taking a photograph. It was not until recently that I discovered that screen-shotting originated from analogue photography and that the technique literally was to hard copy the computer screen using instant Polaroid film. Polaroid even produced a film called Spectra that had the same 4:3 screen ratio of the CRT computer screen. It was an almost cathartic discovery and it reassured me that what I did with *Terra Nullius* both couldn't be illegal but also maybe could be seen equal to Richard Prince photographing the Marlboro Man from magazine advertisements. Overall it affirms my belief that it is not the camera that holds the monopoly on taking photographs.

I wonder if there will be a way of closing the gap between the photographic paper and the painter's white canvas? I am sure the pursuit would result in more hybrid fields within photographic practice. I mean, there is not much left of the collodion process of the 1850s. Today my entire photographic process is digital; my files are moved digitally and are digitally printed with laser or inkjet on anything from canvas to wood. Perhaps all that is left from the birth of photography is the passing of light through a glass lens?

David: Yes, and maybe not even that is left. I suspect more and more photography will become 'photography by other means', but not simply for technical reasons. It seems to me that many of these new hybrid forms have come about in parallel with our shifting relation to history and memory and their effects upon our understanding of ourselves in the present.

Morten: From the way my work has developed I see that it has been defined by few isolated moments and experiences in my life that I keep returning to and reworking. Many of these moments are from my childhood and the beginning of my teenage years and so my work centres upon understanding them. However it has become clear to me that photography on its own falls short, and so my search for a way around it has now taken this hybrid form.

Terra Nullius has arrived from a struggle with the exactness of photography and the fragility of the medium. I have missed that the photographic output is not more physical and does not reveal the human hand that formed it like brushstrokes or pencil marks. I had a long period after studying photography that I spent painting and sculpting. It was both physical and rewarding in a way the darkroom was not, and so I have wanted to recreate the same physical experience when working with photography. Photography is a delicate practise; the surface of the paper is easily prone to scratches and dents; small shifts in exposure turns it too light or too dark and colour temperature can be cool or warm. In many ways photography is a technical endeavour made up of "rules". But I would so much like to be physical and not delicate. With Terra Nullius I have sought a way of working with force, with anger, with splitting and conjoining, and it has almost felt like creating a Frankenstein image, containing horror or beauty.

I work in front of the computer screen and there is no brutality or brute force. The brutality happens within the computer software in zeroes and ones, and so my work process now carries a new paradox. As I attempt to gain independence from the camera I have grown increasingly dependent on the Adobe Corporation. And with the advancement in artificial intelligence technologies, which will untether photography from optics and the physical, I presume I will become even more addicted to the digital and the almighty silicon chip.

David: Photoshop has certainly brought photography closer to painting on some respects, but I guess the question is what kind of painting? Most of the time Photoshop is used to perfect and to idealise images, to eliminate the perceived 'faults' of photography. But of course that's not all it can be used for. I guess since at least the advent of Kodak, artists have been using industrial materials and processes in ways other than those expected by the big imaging corporations. Maybe this too is where the feelings of brutality and transgression come from. Corporate tools being used to serve less than corporate aims.

Morten: In 1995, when studying architecture, I was introduced to futurism and Marcel Duchamp's painting *Nude descending a staircase No. 2.* It would be four years later when studying photography (with you as my teacher) that I learned his painting was influenced by Etienne Jules Marey's chronophotographic studies. It was a significant discovery that widened my world of photography. Marey's work continues to fascinate me but what draws me in the most is his use of photography not as an aesthetic tool, but as a technical tool for his scientific discovery. He did not bother with obtaining an idealised image or with the faults of the image. Later I had a similar experience when seeing Jean-Luc Mylayne's bird photographs at the Photographers Gallery, in 1999. Here his blurred and distorted images with multiple depths of field were obtained through the creation of his own camera lenses and his infinite patience with capturing his bird subjects. There is something fascinating with his approach; it is not the composition of the image or the decisive moment that seem important in the creation of his works, instead it is his interaction with the bird and the memory of it. There is no single focal plane, the image is littered with blurry patches and even the subject is sometimes indistinguishable. Mylane's images do not represent reality as accurately and as detailed as photography usually intended, and at times they appear more like paintings. His photographs are littered with 'faults'.

Terra Nullius has been a long process of accepting the 'faults' of each image and there are a lot. In some ways these faults are connected to guilt or shame and a struggle with the correctness of photography. I have had to make numerous technical compromises that have gone against the grain of my entire technical upbringing. Each image has multiple vanishing points; no single focal plane; shadows pointing in every direction; resized, scaled and shrunken pixels. But throughout the process I have felt that these faults would emerge as a quality in itself. When I painted there was never faults as such; there were many mistakes, bad decisions, weak composition etc. but never the pressure that I feel photography brings of avoiding faults, scratches, blurriness, oversaturation etc. Perhaps if I did realist painting I would subject myself to the same self-criticism that photography can carry with it.

David: In a way photography has always been caught between the perfection it promises and its inevitable faults and failings. Perhaps an acceptance of this is a path to artistic maturity. But what we do with that acceptance is still open to question. Perhaps in pushing the medium in new directions we produce new faults and failings to confront.

APE#121
Morten Barker, Terra Nullius

ISBN 9789490800901
www.artpapereditions.org
www.mortenbarker.com

Editing & graphic design:
Jurgen Maelfeyt (6'56")
Printing: Wilco Art Books,
Amersfoort

With the financial support of
Grosserer L.F. Foghts Fond
and Danish Arts Foundation

DANISH ARTS FOUNDATION